Gratitude Journal

A Year of Living with Intention

Start Date: _____

End Date: _____

If found, please return to:

gratitude

Gratitude is the quality of being thankful and an expression of appreciation for what we have. These feelings remind us that the world has many good things to offer. Numerous studies on positive psychology have demonstrated that a regular gratitude practice can encourage positive emotions, help us savor good experiences, and build resilience to weather difficult moments in life.

Practicing gratitude can also help counter our innate negativity bias, that tendency to fixate on negative experiences while taking for granted positive or neutral aspects of our lives. In this way, a gratitude practice can reframe how we experience the world.

Journaling has also been shown to have a positive effect on mental health and wellbeing. Self-reflection through journaling helps us tune into our inner experience. Through a regular gratitude practice, we cultivate self-awareness, process emotions, and develop insights into our behaviors. Just a few minutes of journaling every day can have a powerful, positive, and long-term effect on our lives.

"Gratitude is not only the greatest of virtues, but the parent of all the others."

—Marcus Tullius Cicero

Benefits of a Consistent Practice

Research has shown that people who follow a consistent gratitude and journaling practice can experience:

- A recognition of the goodness in life
- More positive emotions
- Higher levels of optimism
- Boosted creativity
- Enhanced sensitivity and empathy
- New insights into our own actions and behaviors
- Reduced inclination to social comparisons
- Improved social and romantic relationships
- Better sleep
- Improved health
- Career motivation

How to Begin Your Practice

Each weekly entry includes a gratitude section and a space for free-form journaling. In addition, there are several exercises throughout the journal that aim to develop mindfulness and encourage reflection.

Your Gratitude Practice

Each entry prompts you to list 3 things you are grateful for. You may be grateful for a person, pet, event, opportunity, experience, emotion, or anything else. A key component of your gratitude practice is to be specific about what you are thankful for and why.

Here are a few examples of gratitude affirmations:

- Today, I am thankful for my dog Benji for comforting me when I was feeling down.

- I'm so thankful for my new friend Anna. She knew I was sick today and brought me homemade soup.

- I am grateful for my partner who went above and beyond by organizing a surprise birthday party for me today. What a treat to see all my friends and family together!

- My boss recognized my accomplishments in our meeting today and that made me feel grateful for working with such a supportive team.

Your Journaling Practice

The journaling section is a free form space for additional writing and self-reflection. Whether you are journaling to clear your mind, process emotions, or for self-discovery, there are countless prompts you can find online to meet your writing goals. We have included a few prompts below to help you get started.

Sample journaling prompts:

- What is on your mind today?

- How do you feel at this moment?

- What are you ready to let go of today?

- What emotions are you holding on to?

- What are your core values?

- What do you know today that you didn't know a year ago?

- Who has most impacted your life and why?

- What relationship do you most want to improve and why?

- How do you cope with difficult circumstances?

- What is something you want to achieve and what is a step you can take toward that goal?

"Cultivate the habit of being grateful for every good thing that comes to you, and to give thanks continuously. And because all things have contributed to your advancement, you should include all things in your gratitude."

— Ralph Waldo Emerson

Tips on Developing Your Practice

Find a time to reflect. Journal anytime in the day when you have a few minutes of quiet, undisturbed time. Some people like to journal in the morning to clear their mind before they start their day. Others prefer the evening, using the exercise to unwind and process the events of the day.

Create a habit. Developing a consistent, regular practice will maximize the benefits of gratitude and journaling. Don't worry if you miss an entry every now and then, just pick up where you left off.

Get specific. Being specific in your gratitude practice and remembering the sensations you felt when that good thing happened is key to connecting it to the present moment and deepening the benefits. Instead of writing that you are grateful for your daughter, hone in on a specific quality or event that made you think of her. It might be that you're grateful that your daughter learned how to use her kiddie potty this week, and soon you won't have to deal with dirty diapers.

Today's Date: _____

What three things are you grateful for today?

1. _____
   _____

2. _____
   _____

3. _____
   _____

_____
_____
_____
_____
_____
_____
_____
_____
_____
_____
_____
_____
_____
_____
_____
_____
_____
_____

Today's Date: _____

What three things are you grateful for today?

4. _____
   _____

5. _____
   _____

6. _____
   _____

_____
_____
_____
_____
_____
_____
_____
_____
_____
_____
_____
_____
_____
_____
_____
_____
_____
_____
_____

Today's Date: _____

What three things are you grateful for today?

1. _____

   _____

2. _____

   _____

3. _____

   _____

_____

_____

_____

_____

_____

_____

_____

_____

_____

_____

_____

_____

_____

_____

_____

_____

Relaxation Exercises

Stress and anxiety can easily overwhelm us. These simple exercises are surprisingly effective at calming nerves and reducing stress.

Calming the Body, Calming the Mind

Take a few deep breaths. While slowly breathing in through the nose, say to yourself *calming the body*. While slowly breathing out through the mouth, say *calming the mind*. Repeat this cycle for a few minutes.

Box Breathing

Box breathing is a powerful technique for calming the mind and body. It is an effective method for dealing with a stressful moment, building concentration, and relaxing the body.

Try it:

- Breathe in through your nose while slowly counting to four, then
- Hold your breath while slowly counting to four, then
- Slowly exhale through your mouth while counting to six,
- Pause for four seconds, then repeat the cycle with a four-second inhale
- Follow this pattern for a few minutes.

"Sometimes your joy is the source of your smile, but sometimes your smile can be the source of your joy."

— Thich Nhat Hanh

Body Scan Meditation

Meditation is an ancient practice aimed at quieting the mind from its constant stream of thoughts and feelings. Novice practitioners often focus on their breathing or bodily sensations. A body scan is a great beginner meditation technique.

To do a body scan:

- Find a comfortable seated position that allows you to be relaxed and alert.

- Close your eyes or soften and lower your gaze.

- Take a few slow, deep breaths. Then let your breathing return to its regular rhythm.

- Begin your body scan by focusing your attention on the physical sensations in your feet. Spend a few moments there. Do you feel tingling, vibration, or warmth?

- Slowly move your attention higher up, spending a few moments focusing on the sensations in each area of the body. Proceed to the ankles, then the lower legs, upper legs, and so on, staying in each area for a few breath cycles.

- Continue in this way until you have scanned your entire body.

Today's Date: _____

What three things are you grateful for today?

1. _____
   _____

2. _____
   _____

3. _____
   _____

_____
_____
_____
_____
_____
_____
_____
_____
_____
_____
_____
_____
_____
_____
_____
_____
_____
_____

Core Values as Guiding Stars

Are your actions, decisions, and lifestyle aligned with your true self? A key part of living a fulfilling life involves staying true to our core personal values. Examples of core values include authenticity, compassion, community, creativity, fairness, generosity, justice, kindness, recognition, respect, and spirituality. Find more examples online by searching "core personal values list."

Journal prompt:

- What three values are most important to you? What actions do you take in your daily life that align with each of these values?

- How do your core values align with your lifestyle, career, relationships, and interests?

- Is there anything that makes it difficult for you to live your core values? How might you overcome these barriers to better align your life with your values?

_____

_____

_____

_____

_____

_____

_____

_____

_____

_____

_____

_____

_____

Today's Date: _____

What three things are you grateful for today?

1. _____

   _____

2. _____

   _____

3. _____

   _____

Today's Date: _____

What three things are you grateful for today?

4. _____

    _____

5. _____

    _____

6. _____

    _____

Today's Date: _____

What three things are you grateful for today?

1. _____
   _____

2. _____
   _____

3. _____
   _____

_____
_____
_____
_____
_____
_____
_____
_____
_____
_____
_____
_____
_____
_____
_____
_____
_____
_____
_____

The Power of Kindness

Be kind, often. Research shows that those who perform more acts of kindness for others report higher and more consistent levels of happiness. However, kindness begins with how we view and treat ourselves. Treating ourselves with compassion, especially during difficult or stressful times, is critical to our wellbeing.

Journal prompt:

- What can you do to be more kind to yourself?
- Recall a moment when someone was kind to you. What did they do and how did it make you feel?
- What is one act of kindness you can do for someone else this week?

_____
_____
_____
_____
_____
_____
_____
_____
_____
_____
_____
_____
_____
_____
_____
_____
_____

Today's Date: _____

What three things are you grateful for today?

1. _____

   _____

2. _____

   _____

3. _____

   _____

_____

_____

_____

_____

_____

_____

_____

_____

_____

_____

_____

_____

_____

_____

_____

_____

_____

Today's Date: _____

What three things are you grateful for today?

4. _____
   _____
5. _____
   _____
6. _____
   _____

_____
_____
_____
_____
_____
_____
_____
_____
_____
_____
_____
_____
_____
_____
_____
_____
_____
_____

Today's Date: _____

What three things are you grateful for today?

1. _____
   _____

2. _____
   _____

3. _____
   _____

_____
_____
_____
_____
_____
_____
_____
_____
_____
_____
_____
_____
_____
_____
_____
_____
_____
_____

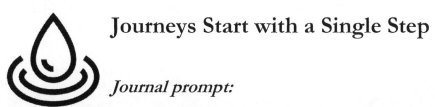

Journeys Start with a Single Step

Journal prompt:

- What one thing are you ready to let go of today?

_____

_____

_____

_____

_____

_____

_____

_____

_____

_____

_____

_____

_____

_____

_____

_____

_____

_____

_____

_____

_____

_____

Today's Date: _____

What three things are you grateful for today?

1. _____
   _____

2. _____
   _____

3. _____
   _____

_____
_____
_____
_____
_____
_____
_____
_____
_____
_____
_____
_____
_____
_____
_____
_____
_____
_____
_____

Today's Date: _____

What three things are you grateful for today?

4. _____
   _____

5. _____
   _____

6. _____
   _____

_____
_____
_____
_____
_____
_____
_____
_____
_____
_____
_____
_____
_____
_____
_____
_____
_____
_____

Today's Date: _____

What three things are you grateful for today?

1. _____

   _____

2. _____

   _____

3. _____

   _____

_____

_____

_____

_____

_____

_____

_____

_____

_____

_____

_____

_____

_____

_____

_____

_____

_____

Reconnecting with Nature

Scientific studies show that time spent in nature can reduce stress and improve symptoms of depression and anxiety. This is why many doctors are now prescribing nature and time outdoors.

Journal prompt:

- Describe your most memorable experience of being in nature.
- What activity can you do outdoors this week?

_____

_____

_____

_____

_____

_____

_____

_____

_____

_____

_____

_____

_____

_____

_____

_____

_____

_____

_____

_____

Today's Date: _____

What three things are you grateful for today?

1. _____
   _____

2. _____
   _____

3. _____
   _____

_____
_____
_____
_____
_____
_____
_____
_____
_____
_____
_____
_____
_____
_____
_____
_____
_____
_____

Today's Date: _____

What three things are you grateful for today?

4. _____
   _____

5. _____
   _____

6. _____
   _____

_____
_____
_____
_____
_____
_____
_____
_____
_____
_____
_____
_____
_____
_____
_____
_____
_____
_____
_____
_____

Reflecting on Personal Growth

Journal prompt:

- Write a letter to your past self.
- What guidance, advice or wisdom would you share with the person you were 5 years ago?

Today's Date: _____

What three things are you grateful for today?

1. _____

_____

2. _____

_____

3. _____

_____

Today's Date: _____

What three things are you grateful for today?

4. _____
   _____

5. _____
   _____

6. _____
   _____

_____
_____
_____
_____
_____
_____
_____
_____
_____
_____
_____
_____
_____
_____
_____
_____
_____
_____
_____
_____

Today's Date: _____

What three things are you grateful for today?

1. _____
   _____

2. _____
   _____

3. _____
   _____

_____
_____
_____
_____
_____
_____
_____
_____
_____
_____
_____
_____
_____
_____
_____
_____
_____
_____
_____
_____
_____

Today's Date: _____

What three things are you grateful for today?

7. _____

   _____

8. _____

   _____

9. _____

   _____

_____
_____
_____
_____
_____
_____
_____
_____
_____
_____
_____
_____
_____
_____
_____
_____
_____
_____
_____

Today's Date: _____

What three things are you grateful for today?

10. _____

_____

11. _____

_____

12. _____

_____

_____

_____

_____

_____

_____

_____

_____

_____

_____

_____

_____

_____

_____

_____

_____

_____

_____

_____

Today's Date: _____

What three things are you grateful for today?

1. _____

   _____

2. _____

   _____

3. _____

   _____

_____
_____
_____
_____
_____
_____
_____
_____
_____
_____
_____
_____
_____
_____
_____
_____
_____
_____
_____
_____
_____

Time Capsule

Journal prompt:

- Write a letter to your future self.
- Five years from now, what do you want to remember about this time in your life? What wisdom would you share?

_____

_____

_____

_____

_____

_____

_____

_____

_____

_____

_____

_____

_____

_____

_____

_____

_____

_____

_____

_____

_____

_____

Today's Date: _____

What three things are you grateful for today?

1. _____
   _____

2. _____
   _____

3. _____
   _____

_____
_____
_____
_____
_____
_____
_____
_____
_____
_____
_____
_____
_____
_____
_____
_____
_____
_____

Today's Date: _____

What three things are you grateful for today?

1. _____
   _____

2. _____
   _____

3. _____
   _____

_____
_____
_____
_____
_____
_____
_____
_____
_____
_____
_____
_____
_____
_____
_____
_____
_____
_____
_____

Today's Date: _____

What three things are you grateful for today?

4. _____

_____

5. _____

_____

6. _____

_____

Strong Fabrics Are Made of Many Threads

Research shows that people with close social ties live longer and are more resilient to stressful events. This is partly due to the benefits of having a strong support network you can rely on during difficult times. However, even loose social connections, like a positive conversation with a stranger, can provide a happiness boost.

Journal prompt:

- What can you do this week to build or strengthen a social connection?
- Is there a damaged relationship you want to improve? What went wrong and how can you begin to repair it?

_____

_____

_____

_____

_____

_____

_____

_____

_____

_____

_____

_____

_____

_____

_____

_____

_____

Today's Date: _____

What three things are you grateful for today?

1. _____

   _____

2. _____

   _____

3. _____

   _____

_____
_____
_____
_____
_____
_____
_____
_____
_____
_____
_____
_____
_____
_____
_____
_____
_____
_____
_____

Today's Date: _____

What three things are you grateful for today?

4. _____
   _____

5. _____
   _____

6. _____
   _____

_____
_____
_____
_____
_____
_____
_____
_____
_____
_____
_____
_____
_____
_____
_____
_____
_____

Today's Date: _____

What three things are you grateful for today?

7. _____
   _____

8. _____
   _____

9. _____
   _____

_____
_____
_____
_____
_____
_____
_____
_____
_____
_____
_____
_____
_____
_____
_____
_____
_____
_____
_____
_____

Today's Date: _____

What three things are you grateful for today?

1. _____

   _____

2. _____

   _____

3. _____

   _____

_____

_____

_____

_____

_____

_____

_____

_____

_____

_____

_____

_____

_____

_____

_____

_____

Today's Date: _____

What three things are you grateful for today?

10. _____

_____

11. _____

_____

12. _____

_____

_____

_____

_____

_____

_____

_____

_____

_____

_____

_____

_____

_____

_____

_____

_____

_____

_____

Today's Date: _____

What three things are you grateful for today?

1. _____
   _____

2. _____
   _____

3. _____
   _____

_____
_____
_____
_____
_____
_____
_____
_____
_____
_____
_____
_____
_____
_____
_____
_____
_____
_____
_____

Change Your Perspective to Uncover Wisdom

Many people feel confident giving advice to others. However, analyzing and finding solutions to our own problems can be much harder. The simple act of switching perspective can help us see the problem from a new angle and better advise ourselves.

Journal prompt:

- In one sentence, write down a challenge that you are facing.
- Now, cue the role reversal. Imagine that a good friend comes to you with the problem you wrote down. What advice would you give this person?

_____

_____

_____

_____

_____

_____

_____

_____

_____

_____

_____

_____

_____

_____

_____

_____

_____

_____

Today's Date: _____

What three things are you grateful for today?

1. _____

_____

2. _____

_____

3. _____

_____

Today's Date: _____

What three things are you grateful for today?

4. _____

   _____

5. _____

   _____

6. _____

   _____

_____

_____

_____

_____

_____

_____

_____

_____

_____

_____

_____

_____

_____

_____

_____

_____

_____

Today's Date: _____

What three things are you grateful for today?

7. _____
   _____

8. _____
   _____

9. _____
   _____

_____
_____
_____
_____
_____
_____
_____
_____
_____
_____
_____
_____
_____
_____
_____
_____
_____
_____
_____

Today's Date: _____

What three things are you grateful for today?

1. _____

   _____

2. _____

   _____

3. _____

   _____

_____

_____

_____

_____

_____

_____

_____

_____

_____

_____

_____

_____

_____

_____

_____

_____

_____

Today's Date: _____

What three things are you grateful for today?

10. _____

_____

11. _____

_____

12. _____

_____

_____

_____

_____

_____

_____

_____

_____

_____

_____

_____

_____

_____

_____

_____

_____

_____

_____

_____

Today's Date: _____

What three things are you grateful for today?

1. _____

   _____

2. _____

   _____

3. _____

   _____

Pay it Forward

Is there a person who often comes up in your gratitude reflections? If so, consider telling them how much they are appreciated. A research study showed that participants who handwrote and personally delivered a letter of gratitude to someone who had supported them experienced significant happiness.

Journal prompt:

- Write a letter to a person you are grateful to have in your life.
- How has this person impacted your life and what has their support meant to you?

_____

_____

_____

_____

_____

_____

_____

_____

_____

_____

_____

_____

_____

_____

_____

_____

_____

_____

Today's Date: _____

What three things are you grateful for today?

1. _____

   _____

2. _____

   _____

3. _____

   _____

_____

_____

_____

_____

_____

_____

_____

_____

_____

_____

_____

_____

_____

_____

_____

_____

_____

_____

Today's Date: _____

What three things are you grateful for today?

4. _____

   _____

5. _____

   _____

6. _____

   _____

_____

_____

_____

_____

_____

_____

_____

_____

_____

_____

_____

_____

_____

_____

_____

_____

Today's Date: _____

What three things are you grateful for today?

1. _____

    _____

2. _____

    _____

3. _____

    _____

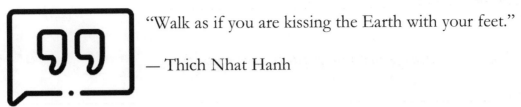

"Walk as if you are kissing the Earth with your feet."

— Thich Nhat Hanh

Today's Date: _____

What three things are you grateful for today?

1. _____

   _____

2. _____

   _____

3. _____

   _____

Today's Date: _____

What three things are you grateful for today?

7. _____
   _____

8. _____
   _____

9. _____
   _____

_____
_____
_____
_____
_____
_____
_____
_____
_____
_____
_____
_____
_____
_____
_____
_____
_____
_____

Today's Date: _____

What three things are you grateful for today?

1. _____

   _____

2. _____

   _____

3. _____

   _____

_____
_____
_____
_____
_____
_____
_____
_____
_____
_____
_____
_____
_____
_____
_____
_____
_____
_____

Enhancing the Richness of Life

Sharing experiences with others makes those moments feel richer to us. One study showed that chocolate tastes better when we are tasting it at the same time as someone else. Many of us have experienced this firsthand: wishing a friend or partner were there to share in a delicious meal, a momentous occasion, or a beautiful sunset.

Journal prompt:

- What is an experience that you want to share with someone else?
- What do you need to do to make it happen?

Today's Date: _____

What three things are you grateful for today?

1. _____
   _____
2. _____
   _____
3. _____
   _____

Today's Date: _____

What three things are you grateful for today?

4. _____

_____

5. _____

_____

6. _____

_____

_____

_____

_____

_____

_____

_____

_____

_____

_____

_____

_____

_____

_____

_____

_____

_____

_____

Today's Date: _____

What three things are you grateful for today?

1. _____
   _____

2. _____
   _____

3. _____
   _____

Today's Date: _____

What three things are you grateful for today?

7. _____
   _____

8. _____
   _____

9. _____
   _____

_____
_____
_____
_____
_____
_____
_____
_____
_____
_____
_____
_____
_____
_____
_____
_____
_____
_____

Today's Date: _____

What three things are you grateful for today?

1. _____

   _____

2. _____

   _____

3. _____

   _____

Today's Date: _____

What three things are you grateful for today?

10. _____

_____

11. _____

_____

12. _____

_____

_____

_____

_____

_____

_____

_____

_____

_____

_____

_____

_____

_____

_____

_____

_____

_____

_____

_____

Today's Date: _____

What three things are you grateful for today?

1. _____

   _____

2. _____

   _____

3. _____

   _____

Today's Date: _____

What three things are you grateful for today?

13. _____

_____

14. _____

_____

15. _____

_____

_____

_____

_____

_____

_____

_____

_____

_____

_____

_____

_____

_____

_____

_____

_____

_____

_____

_____

Today's Date: _____

What three things are you grateful for today?

16. _____

_____

17. _____

_____

18. _____

_____

_____

_____

_____

_____

_____

_____

_____

_____

_____

_____

_____

_____

_____

_____

_____

_____

_____

Today's Date: _____

What three things are you grateful for today?

1. _____
   _____

2. _____
   _____

3. _____
   _____

_____
_____
_____
_____
_____
_____
_____
_____
_____
_____
_____
_____
_____
_____
_____
_____
_____
_____
_____
_____

Gratitude
Journal

A Year of Living with Intention

Time to Order a New Journal

Order a new copy here: **www.citizenupgrade.com/gratitude**

Made in the USA
Coppell, TX
06 December 2021

67294243R00049